The Sweet Life

This is a book of favorites. We all have them, yours, mine and ours. That special something that may transport you to a different place in time, bringing back memories of a special occasion, or just a sweet moment shared with a friend over a cup of coffee. For me, food is intrinsically linked with love and connection. It pleases me to make someone's favorite and see their eyes light up with anticipation of that first bite. It is soul-satisfying to give that happiness to people. So, what follows is a beginning, a small compilation of pastries and desserts that are favorites to many people I've had the pleasure to bake for over the years. Much love and gratitude goes out to all those whom have given me their support and encouragement here in Ojai, with a special nod to the Thacher community in particular. Thanks to my darling family— Jude, Ashley, Garner and Graham for always giving me their love. And a very special thanks to my photographer Richard Lancaster, my real life James Bond! Let the baking begin...

Table of Contents

"Life is short, eat dessert first!"

– anonymous

Some helpful tips for a successful bake!

First, read the recipe through to the end. It may sound silly but will help you with time management.

Second, gather all your ingredients and needed equipment together before you start. In the culinary profession this is called *mise en place* which translates to everything in its place! Probably the most important aspect to begin your baking.

Third, preheat your oven and prepare your pans for baking.

Fourth, pay special attention to how your batter looks while in the mixing process! Scrape down sides and bottom of mixing bowl— eggs and butter both like to gather at the bottom and rim of bowls, whether it's cookie dough, mousse or cakes. This is very important and will ensure an even end result.

And lastly, take your time and have fun. This is what it's all about!

Morning Pastries to start the day....

Spiced Apple Puffs

This twist on the classic popover invokes memories of childhood cinnamon toast.

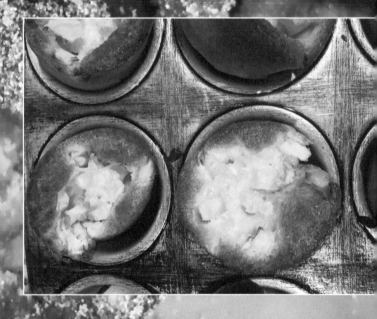

Method

In a medium mixing bowl combine dry ingredients with a whisk. Pour in milk and slightly beaten eggs, whisk to combine and then quickly add melted butter and whisk in until incorporated and no big lumps of flour are visible.

Pour batter into muffin tins halfway full and sprinkle diced apple on top, distributing evenly.

Bake for 20 minutes at 375 degrees then turn pan around in oven and bake another 10-15 minutes at 350 degrees.

Make sure to lower oven when turning pan halfway through baking or the puffs will get too dark.

Remove from oven and let cool a couple of minutes.

Meanwhile melt butter and prepare a shallow bowl with sugar and spices, stirring in cinnamon and cardamom until mixed through.

While puffs are still warm and in the tins brush tops liberally with the melted butter and then toss puffs in the sugar and spice mixture to coat, making sure to sprinkle sugar into the cavity made on the bottom while baking. The puffs should release from the pan quite easily but if they stick run a knife around the sides and pull up with fingertips with a slight twisting motion.

These are best eaten the same day as baked. Makes 10-12 puffs.

Spiced Apple Puffs

Preheat oven to 375°
Tools needed
Muffin tin liberally greased or sprayed with Pam
Pastry brush

Ingredients for batter:

1 ounce melted butter
3 eggs - slightly beaten
1 c.milk
¼ t. salt
½ T. sugar
1 c. flour
1 apple peeled and diced

Ingredients for topping:
1 ounce melted butter - hot!
1 c. sugar
1 t. ground cinnamon
½ t. ground cardamom

Blueberry Ginger Scones

Blueberry Ginger Scones

Measure out the dry ingredients, and mix together:
3 cups all purpose flour- not sifted
1 T. Baking powder
½ cup granulated sugar
½ t. Baking soda
½ t. salt
½ cup quick or old fashioned oats
Add: 6 ounces chilled unsalted butter, cut in cubes.

Either with a pastry cutter, fork, or your fingers, cut in the butter to the dry
  ingredients until butter is no bigger than the size of a small pea. Then
  slowly pour wet ingredients over dry ingredients mixing with a fork until it
  almost comes together.

Mix together wet ingredients:
⅓ cup half and half, or more if needed
1 egg, lightly beaten
1 t. vanilla

When mixture is almost sticking together into a dough you will add the
  blueberries and chopped candied ginger:
2 cups fresh blueberries
½ cup chopped candied ginger

Continue to lightly mix until fruit and ginger are incorporated. On two
  parchment paper lined baking sheets scoop out scones, I use a three ounce
  ice cream scoop to ensure they're the same size but a large spoon works just
  as well. This recipe makes 12 scones. Bake 18-20 minutes in 375 degree
  oven until lightly browned around edges and softly firm to the touch. If
  making smaller scones set timer for 10-12 minutes and check for doneness
  until firm.

Variation: Mixed berry scones

Follow recipe for blueberry ginger scones
but substitute 2 cups mixed black, blue and
raspberries instead.

Bake as directed for Blueberry ginger scones

Variations on a scone....

Maple scones (nuts optional)
Basic scone recipe (see previous page) omitting blueberries and ginger
If using nuts omit oats and substitute 1 cup chopped walnuts or pecans
  instead.

To liquid ingredients add 1 Tablespoon maple extract
Bake 18-20 minutes as directed at 375°, let cool and dip scones in warm
  maple icing.
Sprinkle with chopped nuts (optional)

Maple icing:
In small saucepan melt 2 ounces unsalted butter and 1/2 cup dark brown
  sugar, cook, stirring constantly for about one minute or until mixture is
  smooth and starts to bubble.

Remove from heat and add 2 teaspoons maple extract and ¼ cup very hot
  water, whisk until smooth and then stir in 2 cups sifted powdered sugar,
  whisk until smooth adding a few drops of hot water to make a smooth
  somewhat loose icing.

Dip scones quickly in icing before it gets cold, holding scones one at a time
  upside down and submerge top, shake off excess and place right side up on
  baking sheet or baker's rack to cool.
Sprinkle with nuts if desired.

Walnut Streusel Coffee Cake

Method

In Kitchen Aid with paddle attachment cream together the butter and sugar until light and fluffy. Add eggs one at a time, scraping down sides and bottom of bowl, and beat until incorporated. Add vanilla, buttermilk, and orange zest and juice. Mix on low speed for one minute then add all dry ingredients (no need to sift) mix on low speed for 30 seconds. Scrape down sides and bottom of bowl then continue to mix on medium speed for one minute. Evenly spread batter in prepared pan and top with streusel, sprinkling evenly over top, then with tips of fingers pat streusel into batter to create pockets of crumb mixture throughout. Bake 50-60 minutes until toothpick inserted in middle comes out clean. Cool at least 15 minutes and then drizzle with icing.

Icing; 2 cups sifted powdered sugar, 1t. vanilla, 1/3 to 1/2 c. hot water, whisk until smooth.

Walnut Streusel Coffee Cake

Preheat oven to 350°
Butter and lightly flour a 9 by 12 inch pan, set aside.

Make streusel topping:
4 ounces salted butter
1 cup dark brown sugar
1 cup all purpose flour
1 t. cinnamon
8 ounces chopped walnuts

Melt butter and mix remaining ingredients in medium sized bowl, pour butter over top and mix with a fork until a crumbly mixture has formed.
Set aside.

Coffee cake batter:
8 ounces unsalted butter
2 cups granulated sugar
4 eggs
2 cups buttermilk
1 t. vanilla
Zest and juice of one orange
5 cups all purpose flour
2 t. Baking powder
¾ t. Baking soda
½ t. Salt

Tray Bakes and Cookies

Apricot Granola Bars

Apricot Granola Bars

Method

First prepare a 9 by 12 in. pan by spraying lightly with Pam and line bottom with parchment paper, set aside.

In large mixing bowl combine all the dry ingredients and mix with your hands, breaking up any lumps. Pour melted butter over top and toss with a fork until mixture is crumbly, you may need to use your hands to make sure everything has absorbed the butter. Sprinkle two thirds of the mixture into pan and press down evenly making sure that there are no open spots where preserves can seep through. Next, dot preserves over the granola base in pan and spread evenly using an offset spatula. Sprinkle remaking granola mixture over top and press down lightly. Bake at 350 for about 35 minutes or until top and sides are lightly brown. Cool completely before cutting, these are easier to cut if you refrigerate them for an hour or so. They're a great treat for children's lunchboxes or dress it up a little by serving them warm with a scoop of vanilla ice cream on top. Yields 2 dozen bars.

Preheat oven to 350°
Ingredients:
8 ounces unsalted butter-melted
2 cups all purpose flour
2 ½ cups old fashioned oats
1 cup dark brown sugar
½ t. baking powder
½ t. salt
1- 15 ounce jar apricot preserves

Note: for a healthier version I use organic reduced sugar preserves or fruit spread also works fine!

Double Chocolate Brownies

Double chocolate brownies

Method

Prepare a 9 by 13 inch pan by spraying lightly with Pam and line bottom with parchment paper, lightly spray top of paper with Pam and set aside.

In a large heat proof bowl melt chocolate and butter over a pan of simmering hot water, stirring often until smooth. Remove from heat and cool slightly for about 15 minutes. Add sugar, vanilla and salt and whisk to combine— at this point it will look grainy, don't worry! Add the 4 eggs and whisk until smooth. Sift flour over top and stir into mixture until incorporated and then stir in the chocolate chips. Spoon into pan and spread evenly into the four corners. Bake at 350° 25-30 minutes, until set but not too firm. Chill before cutting.

Yields 2 dozen fudge brownies.

Variation: Cookie and cream brownies

Follow recipe above, omitting chocolate chips and instead fold in 15 crushed Oreo cookies that have been tossed with 1 ounce melted butter.

Bake as directed above.

Preheat oven to 350°

Ingredients:
4 ounces unsweetened bakers chocolate
8 ounces unsalted butter
½ t. salt
2 cups granulated sugar
1 cup all purpose flour
4 eggs
1 t. vanilla
½ t. salt
2 cups semisweet chocolate chips

Dessert is probably the most important stage of the meal, since it will be the last thing your guests remember before they pass out all over the table.
William Powell

Preheat oven to 350°

Spray 9 by 13 inch nonstick baking pan with Pam spray and press the
  following cookie crumb mixture into bottom of pan:

2 cups Oreo cookie crumbs tossed with
2 Tablespoons melted butter
Set aside pan and make brownies -
4 ounces unsweetened bakers chocolate
8 ounces butter
2 c. sugar
1 c. a.p. flour
4 eggs
1 t. vanilla extract

*Cheesecake
Brownies*

Melt chocolate and butter in heat proof bowl over simmering hot water,
  stirring occasionally until melted.
Remove from heat and cool slightly then whisk in sugar, eggs and vanilla until
  blended well.
Sift flour into chocolate mixture and stir in until free from lumps.
Poor into prepared pan and smooth evenly into corners with spatula or back of
  large spoon. Set aside and prepare cheesecake top.

8 ounces softened cream cheese
¼ c. sugar
½ t. vanilla
1 egg

In mixing bowl with paddle attachment or by hand beat cream cheese until
  smooth. Add sugar, vanilla and egg and beat until incorporated.
Mixture should be smooth and satiny in texture.
Fill piping bag with cheesecake mixture and pipe 4 or 5 strips across
  brownies, or if you don't have a piping bag you can dollop mixture onto top
  of brownies creating your own pattern.
Using the back of a knife, draw cheesecake mixture through brownies
  alternating directions to form a feathered effect.
Bake for 35 minutes at 350°.
Chill completely before cutting.
Yields 2 dozen brownies.

Chocolate Cherry Chews

Method

In mixing bowl cream together the butter, sugar and vanilla until light and fluffy.

Stir in the flour and salt, mix just until crumbly, then add the cherries and chocolate.

Stir just until dough comes together and flour is incorporated. Pat evenly into the 9+9 pan and sprinkle top with cinnamon sugar. Bake as directed for 30-35 minutes, edges and top should be lightly browned.

Remove from oven and cut into squares before cool, they're much easier to cut when warm.

Yield 16 pieces.

These keep well in a tin for weeks!

Chocolate Cherry Chews

**Preheat oven to 325°
30-35 minutes**

**Line a 9 by 9 inch pan
with parchment paper
and spray lightly with
Pam, set aside**

Ingredients:
**8 ounces unsalted butter,
softened**
1 cup granulated sugar
1 t. vanilla extract
**2 ¼ cups all purpose
flour**
½ t. salt
**½ cup dried tart cherries
soaked in 1 T. orange
juice**
**1 cup chopped dark
chocolate or chocolate
chips**
1 T. sugar mixed with
**⅛ t. cinnamon to
sprinkle on top**

Ojai Orangies

These are a favorite of citrus lovers everywhere,
I substitute pixie tangerines for the oranges during their season
so feel free to play around !
Thanks to Ginger Maxwell for sharing this recipe.

Method

Zest and juice of one large orange or 2 tangerines. Reserve half for frosting.

Cream together butter and sugar until light and fluffy, add eggs one at a time beating well after each, add half of the orange juice and zest reserving the other half for the frosting. Stir in vanilla and salt then add the flour and mix until incorporated. Spoon into prepared pan and spread evenly into corners with a spatula. Bake 325° for 30 minutes, should be lightly browned. Remove from oven and prick all over top with a fork. Pour frosting over top and spread evenly with spatula. Cool completely before cutting. Yield 16 squares.

Frosting; Combine 1½ cups sifted powdered sugar with remaining orange juice and zest and a drop of vanilla.

Whisk together until smooth, adding a few drops of water if needed.

Note: these keep well for several days covered at room temp. or in the refrigerator.

Ojai Orangies

**Preheat oven to 350°
for 30 minutes**

**9 by 9 square pan, lined
with parchment paper
and lightly sprayed with
Pam**

Ingredients:
6 ounces unsalted butter
1 ½ cups granulated sugar
3 eggs
1 ⅛ cup all purpose flour
½ t. salt
1 t. vanilla

Many years ago, Krishnamurti
told a friend,
"If I had nowhere to go in the world,
I would come to Ojai.
I would sit under an orange tree;
it would shade me from the sun,
and I could live on the fruit."

Baklava

*This is actually a lot easier than you think,
just take your time...*

Method

To make the baklava; place all dry ingredients in a bowl and mix together thoroughly, set aside. Melt the butter, you want to keep it hot so if it cools during the assembly process just return to heat for a few seconds. Unwrap phyllo dough and unroll gently until it is a flat block, cover with clean dish towel when not working with it as this prevents it from drying out. Working quickly, place a sheet of the phyllo dough on baking tray and brush lightly with butter, repeat this step until half the dough is used, trimming overhanging edges as you go. Spread the nut mixture evenly over dough and press down lightly; then resume layering the dough brushed with butter until all the dough is used up. I take the trimmings and use these also, patching them together to make a full sheet, just don't do it on the top because it will spoil the look and make it hard to cut. Brush top completely with butter. With a sharp Chef's knife cut dough into ten strips across being careful not to cut all the way through to the bottom. Then cut on a diagonal across 6 strips, this will make a nice diamond pattern. Don't worry, there will be some pieces around the corners that aren't full diamond shape, these are always my favorite part! Bake in low oven: 275° for an hour and 15 minutes.

While baking make the syrup as follows:

Baklava

**Preheat oven to 275°
for 1 hour and 15
minutes**
**9 by 13 inch baking pan,
lightly sprayed with Pam**
**Special equipment- pastry
brush**
Ingredients:
4 cups ground walnuts
½ cup granulated sugar
**½ cup graham cracker
crumbs**
2 t. cinnamon
⅛ t. cloves
8 ounces unsalted butter
1 package phyllo dough

Syrup:
2 cups sugar
1 ½ cup water
¼ cup honey
½ orange, cut into slices
1 stick cinnamon
1 t. lemon juice

Place all ingredients into medium saucepan except lemon juice and stir until sugar and honey is dissolved. Bring to a boil over high heat and then turn down to medium heat, it should be boiling lightly for about 15-20 minutes. Strain through sieve pressing the juice out of the orange slices and add lemon juice. Set aside in a pourable container such as a pitcher or a Pyrex measuring cup.

When baklava is done let cool for five minutes after removing from oven. Pour syrup slowly and evenly over baklava making sure syrup covers every single piece or it will be dry. Let cool completely on rack before going back and cutting through again all the way to the bottom. Lift out pieces with a small offset spatula for best results. Yields about 40 pieces. Store in covered container.

Chocolate Chip Cookies

Everyone's favorite cookie

Chocolate Chip Cookies

Method

Cream together the butter, both sugars and vanilla extract in mixing bowl with paddle attachment or a large bowl with a wooden spoon.

Add eggs one at a time, mixing well each time and continue until light and fluffy. Stir in the flour, salt and baking soda, making sure to sift baking soda into flour before mixing.

Add the chocolate chips and stir in just until all the dough has chips throughout. Take care to scrape sides and bottom of the bowl if using a kitchen aid as batter often collects in these places and doesn't get mixed in well.

Spoon dough onto parchment lined baking pans, I use a small ice cream scoop and this works perfectly for even sized cookies. 12-15 cookies balls per sheet .

Bake at 350° 12-13 minutes or until edges are lightly browned.

Remove from oven and let cool a minute before transferring them to a wire mesh cooling rack. These cookies will spread so leave lots of space between them on baking sheet!

Yields about 4 1/2 dozen.

12 ounces (3 sticks) unsalted butter
1 cup granulated sugar
1 cup packed dark brown sugar
4 eggs
3 ½ cups all purpose flour
1 t. baking soda
1 t. salt
1 ½ t. vanilla extract
20 ounces (2 bags) dark chocolate chips

Snickerdoodles

*Perfect for an afternoon snack and not too sweet,
these treats can't be beat!*

Snickerdoodles

Method

Preheat oven to 350 degrees, line two baking pans with parchment paper and set aside

Cream together butter and sugar with vanilla extract until light and fluffy.

Add eggs one at a time and mix well. Sift baking soda, cream of tartar and salt into flour (there's no need to sift the flour) and stir until dry ingredients are incorporated.

Place reserved sugar and cinnamon into a bowl and mix well.

Scoop out cookie dough into balls and roll in cinnamon sugar, place 12 each on baking sheet and lightly press down each ball.

Bake 10-15 minutes until edges are lightly browned. Cool on wire rack.

Yields 2 1/2 to 3 dozen.

Ingredients:

8 ounces unsalted butter-softened
1 ½ cups sugar
2 eggs
1 t. vanilla extract
3 cups a.p. flour
1 t. soda
½ t. salt
¾ t. cream of tartar
2 t. cinnamon + 1 c. of sugar to roll dough in

It is the
Little things
In life that
Can make
You smile
Like an idiot
-b.q.

Ginger Molasses Cookies

Perfect with a glass of milk!

Ginger Molasses Cookies

Method

Cream together butter and sugar in kitchen aid with paddle attachment or in a large mixing bowl with a wooden spoon.

Add eggs one at a time mixing well, then add the molasses and vanilla, scraping down side and bottom of bowl to mix evenly.

Sift the spices, salt and baking soda into the flour and stir all into the molasses mixture.

Prepare a bowl with the extra sugar.

Spoon dough into balls and roll each one completely in sugar, place 12 to a baking sheet lightly press down each cookie on baking sheet.

Bake 10-15 minutes until a rich, spicy smell and crisp edges are apparent. Cool on wire rack.

Yields about 3 1/2 to 4 dozen.

Preheat oven to 350°

Line 2 cookie sheets with parchment paper and set aside

Ingredients:
6 ounces unsalted butter, softened
2 cups sugar
2 eggs
½ cup molasses
4 c. a.p. flour
1 T. ground ginger
1 T. baking soda
¾ T. cinnamon
1 t. cloves
¾ t. salt
1 t. vanilla extract
Extra sugar (about 1 1/2 cup) for rolling

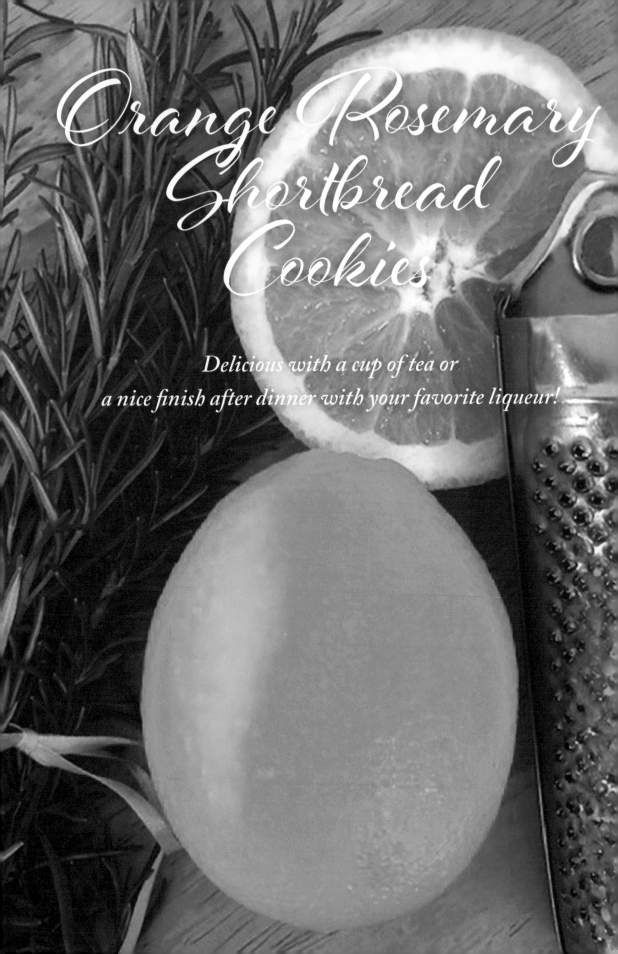

Method

In mixing bowl cream together butter and sugar until light and fluffy, add vanilla, orange zest and juice and continue beating until incorporated.

Stir in flour, salt and rosemary just until mixed, form dough into 2 long round bars and wrap in plastic.

Refrigerate at least 2 hours.

Remove plastic from bars and slice into 1/4 inch circles.

Place cookies on parchment lined cookie sheets one inch apart and sprinkle lightly with sugar.

Bake about 10-15 minutes until lightly browned around edges.

Remove from pan and let cookies cool on baker's rack. Store in tin or airtight container.

Orange Rosemary Shortbread Cookies

Preheat oven to 300°

Ingredients:
8 ounces unsalted butter
1 c. granulated sugar
1 t. vanilla extract
1 t. orange zest
1 t. orange juice
½ t. salt
½ t. fresh Rosemary, chopped fine
2 ¼ c. all purpose flour
extra sugar for dusting tops

A great cookie for afternoon tea!

Lemon Lavender Shortbread Cookies

Follow recipe for Orange Rosemary shortbread cookies, omitting orange zest and juice and fresh rosemary.

Replace with 1 t. grated lemon zest, 1 t. lemon juice and ¾ t. fresh culinary lavender flowers, chopped.

Bake as directed in previous recipe. Enjoy!

Special Desserts & Cakes

"No sooner had the warm liquid mixed with the crumbs touched my palate than a shudder ran through me and I stopped, intent upon the extraordinary thing that was happening to me. An exquisite pleasure had invaded my senses, something isolated, detached, with no suggestion of its origin."- Marcel Proust

Banana Brownie Pillows

Light and satisfying, you're sure to dream about them once you've had one!

Method

Lightly spray a 9 inch square pan with Pam and set aside

This recipe has a few parts. It is fairly simple once you break it down so don't be intimidated. Basically it's like the best custard pie you've ever had in bar form. It's a great way to use up brownies, just wrap up 3 or 4 of them and save them to use when making this recipe. Here we go….

For bottom crust:

Combine the Oreo crumbs with melted butter until mixed together and press into bottom of the 9 in. pan and bake 5 minutes in a 350° oven.

Remove from oven and let cool completely.

When cool, slice the bananas and brownies and layer alternating on top of crust. Pour hot custard over all and spread evenly with spatula, making sure to cover all the sliced banana and brownies.

Custard for banana brownie pillows:

In a cereal sized bowl combine the 3 T. cornstarch with half the sugar and mix well so there are no lumps. Whisk in 1/2 a cup of the low-fat milk until smooth and then whisk in the egg yolks again until smooth. Set aside.

In 1 quart saucepan combine the other half of the sugar with 1½ c. of the low-fat milk. Stir to combine and set on medium high heat stirring occasionally to prevent sticking and burning. When milk starts to come to a boil quickly whisk in egg yolk mixture and cook

Banana Brownie Pillows

Preheat oven to 300°

Ingredients:
1 ½ ounces melted butter
2 c. Oreo cookie crumbs
1-2 bananas
3-4 brownies
2 c. low fat milk
½ c. granulated sugar
3 T. cornstarch
2 egg yolks
1 t. vanilla extract
1 c. whipping cream
2 T. powdered sugar
Chocolate shavings or
  sprinkles for top

stirring constantly until thickened, large bubbles will begin to break on the surface, this should only take a minute or two. Stir in vanilla and pour over your banana brownie mixture as directed previously. Let this all cool in the refrigerator at least an hour. Whip the 1 cup of whipping cream with the powdered sugar until soft peaks form and spread evenly over top. Sprinkle with chocolate shavings or sprinkles and cut into squares. Remove from pan with offset spatula and enjoy!

Some More Bars

Just like the campfire favorite these will

leave you wanting "some more"!

There are three parts to this recipe, gather your ingredients and then proceed step by step.

Special tools:
9+9 inch square pan
hand held culinary torch.

Start with the bottom layer, the graham cracker crust. Mix the first 4 ingredients together well and press into the 9 by 9 inch pan that has been lightly sprayed with Pam. Bake at 350° for 5-7 minutes until edges are lightly browned. Remove and let cool while preparing ganache for second layer.

Method:

Ganache:

In a medium saucepan heat the heavy cream over medium high heat until it comes to a scald, it will start to rise up the sides of the pan.

Quickly turn off heat and pour the 2 c. chocolate chips into the cream whisking vigorously until mixture is smooth and glossy.

Pour ganache over graham cracker crust and spread evenly with a spatula. Refrigerate at least one hour before preparing the final layer of marshmallow.

Continued on page 53

Some More Bars

Ingredients:
2 c. Graham cracker crumbs
4 oz. melted butter
¼ c. dark brown sugar
¼ t. baking powder
1 c. heavy cream
2 c. dark chocolate chips
1 c. granulated sugar
½ c. hot water
⅛ c. light corn syrup
½ Tablespoon powdered gelatin
1 t. vanilla
¼ t. lemon juice

"These are like a bite of heaven...."
-Luke S.

To make the marshmallow:

In a kitchen aid bowl with whisk attachment (or a medium sized bowl with electric beaters) dissolve the gelatin with 1/4 c. of the hot water, whisk thoroughly and set aside.

Place sugar, corn syrup and the other 1/4 cup of water in a small saucepan and stir to dissolve the sugar. Place on high heat and bring to a boil, do not stir, until hard ball stage is reached— 250° with a candy thermometer or you can test it by dropping a small amount into a glass of cold water. If it forms into a ball it's ready.

Quickly pour syrup into gelatin mixture—it will be very hot—and start beating on medium low speed adding lemon juice and vanilla. After a minute or two scrape bowl to ensure mixture is being evenly incorporated and continue to beat on medium speed for a few minutes.

At this point it will look milky and quite runny but don't be discouraged, it will come together to be light and fluffy. Increase speed as mixture cools down and thickens, beat until soft peaks form, about 7-10 minutes total.

When marshmallow has achieved desired consistency it is ready. Remove pan with crust and ganache mixture from refrigerator. Spoon marshmallow over top, using an offset spatula smooth evenly into corners, completely covering the ganache mixture.

This is much easier to do when chocolate is completely set so give yourself enough time when making this dessert, it will be worth it.

Now for toasting the top.

Using a hand held culinary torch, turn the flame on high and holding the torch about 10 inches away from pan start toasting your marshmallow top by evenly moving the flame side to side as it brown; if this doesn't happen easily then move your torch a bit closer until the flame browns the top but doesn't catch it on fire. (Remember those charcoal marshmallows around the campfire? You don't want that!)

Voila! Cut into squares and enjoy. These keep in the refrigerator for a few days; you may want to re-toast the top but it's not necessary.

Method:

Chop chocolate and place in a heat-proof bowl.

In a small saucepan combine sugar and water, stir to dissolve sugar and place over high heat to bring to a boil. Continue to boil syrup for a couple of minutes but don't let it start to carmelize; it should be pale in color and not thick!

Pour immediately over chocolate and whisk until chocolate is melted, continue to whisk in egg yolks and vanilla. Let cool to room temperature.

Whip the 2 c. cream until soft peaks form, cream should hold its shape in mounds but not peaks, over whipping the cream will affect the texture.

With a rubber spatula, fold in 1/3 of the cream into the chocolate until barely mixed and then add the rest of the cream, folding in gently until there are no streaks of cream left.

Chill before scooping into parfait glasses.

Top with sweetened whipped cream and chocolate shavings.

Serves 6.

"I can resist anything but temptation"

– Mae West

Dark Chocolate Mousse

Ingredients:

8 ounces good quality dark chocolate
½ c. filtered water
½ c. sugar
4 egg yolks
2 c. heavy whipping cream
1 t. vanilla extract

Topping:

1 c. heavy whipping cream
3 T. powdered sugar

Whip cream with powdered sugar until thickened and soft peaks form

Chocolate shavings or sprinkles (optional)

Butterscotch Pudding

Butterscotch Pudding

Method:

In a small bowl combine the cornstarch with 1/4 c. of the dark brown sugar, stir to combine thoroughly. Whisk in 1/4 c. of the milk and the 3 egg yolks until smooth. Set aside.

In a medium saucepan over medium high heat melt the butter and add the remaining dark brown sugar, stirring constantly with a whisk to cook the sugar and bring out the flavor for about one minute. Add the remaining milk, still whisking constantly until sugar dissolves. Heat the milk mixture, stirring occasionally, until it begins to simmer, temper the reserved egg/cornstarch mixture by stirring in a little of the heated milk into the bowl and then pour it all back into the saucepan, whisking constantly over heat until bubbles start to plop on the surface and pudding thickens.

Remove from heat and stir in the salt, vanilla and whiskey. Pour into parfait glasses and let chill completely, at least 2 hours. Top with sweetened whipped cream and crushed Oreo cookies.

Note: the secret to this smooth rich pudding is NOT to let the milk boil before adding the egg and cornstarch mixture. It may be tedious to stand over the stove whisking for a few minutes but it will ensure better results. The pudding has a tendency to separate if the milk is heated too quickly!

Serves 6

Parfait glasses or ramekins

Ingredients:

2 ounces unsalted butter
1 c. dark brown sugar
4 T. cornstarch
3 egg yolks
1 t. vanilla
2 t. scotch whiskey
⅛ t. salt

Topping:
1 c. heavy whipping cream
3 T. powdered sugar

Whip cream with powdered sugar until thickened and soft peaks form

6 Oreo cookies

Red Velvet Cake

Another old fashioned treat that comforts and satisfies

Method:

Sift together dry ingredients and set aside.

In Kitchen Aid with paddle attachment or large mixing bowl with electric beaters cream together softened butter and sugar on low speed until mixed. Increase speed to medium and continue to beat until mixture is pale yellow and creamy. Add eggs one at a time beating thoroughly until light and fluffy, taking care to scrape down sides and bottom with a rubber spatula halfway through to ensure even mixing.

Reduce speed to low and add half the dry ingredients, mix until no flour is visible. Slowly add all the buttermilk and red food coloring continuing to mix on low, scraping down sides and bottom of bowl until liquid is incorporated into the batter.

Add remaining flour and mix on low until flour is absorbed. Scrape down bowl again, add apple cider vinegar and vanilla mixing on low speed. Increase speed to medium and beat 2-3 minutes until batter is light and fluffy. Scoop out into muffin tins lined with cupcake papers or into two greased and parchment lined 9 inch pans.

Bake cupcakes for 15-20 minutes at 350° and for 9" cake layers bake 25-30 minutes. To test for doneness, insert a wooden toothpick or skewer in center of cake and it should come out clean. This particular cake is easy to overbake so be watchful the last few minutes of baking to ensure a beautifully moist cake.

When cool, ice with creamy vanilla buttercream.

Red Velvet Cake

Pre-heat oven to 350°

Yield 2 ½ dozen cupcakes or 9" 2 layer cake

Ingredients:
8 ounces unsalted butter-softened
1 ½ c. sugar
2 ounces red food color
3 T. dark cocoa powder
¼ t. salt
2 eggs
1 c. buttermilk
1 t. apple cider vinegar
1 t. vanilla extract
1 c. cake flour
1 ½ c. all purpose flour
1 ½ t. baking soda

Creamy Vanilla Buttercream

Homemade Vanilla Extract

Creamy Vanilla Buttercream

Method:

This versatile frosting can be used for red velvet and tender butter cake as well as dark chocolate cake.

Cream together butter and cream cheese in kitchen aid mixing bowl with paddle attachment, or by hand in a large bowl with a wooden spoon.

Add 1 1/2 to 2 pounds of sifted powdered sugar depending on how much frosting you want.

Mix on low or by hand until butter and cream cheese is becoming absorbed into the sugar and slowly add enough half and half just until mixture starts to come together around paddle or spoon.

Increase speed to high and beat a minute or two, stop and scrape down sides and bottom of bowl making sure there are no lumps.

Add vanilla and more half and half if needed, a little at a time, continue to beat until the consistency is smooth and easy to spread.

Keeps well in an airtight container in the refrigerator for 7 days, bring to room temperature before using.

Frosts one 9" double or triple layer cake.

Ingredients:

4 ounces unsalted butter softened
4 ounces cream cheese- softened
1 ½ to 2 pounds powdered sugar- sifted
¼ c. half and half, more if needed
1 t. vanilla extract

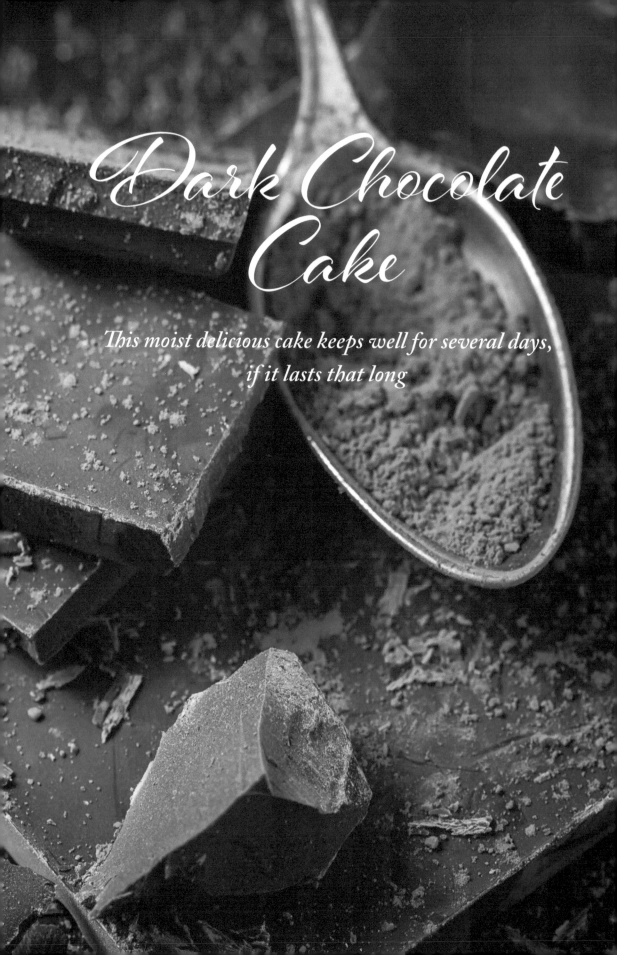

Dark Chocolate Cake

This moist delicious cake keeps well for several days, if it lasts that long

Method:

Sift together all dry ingredients and place in Kitchen Aid mixing bowl with paddle attachment or large mixing bowl with electric beaters.

On low speed slowly add the hot coffee and water followed by the buttermilk and canola oil.

Stop and scrape down sides and bottom of bowl with rubber spatula.

Continue to mix on low, adding eggs and vanilla until they are incorporated, then turn up speed to medium high and beat 2-3 minutes.

Divide batter into 3 9" pans which have been lined with parchment paper and lightly greased.

Bake at 350° about 25-30 minutes or until cake feels set when lightly touched.

Cool completely before icing with creamy vanilla buttercream or dark chocolate buttercream.

Enjoy!

Moist & Delicious Dark Chocolate Cake

Pre-heat oven to 350°

Makes a 3-layer 9" cake

Ingredients:

3 c. sugar
1 ½ c. all purpose flour
1 c. cake flour
1 ½ c. dark cocoa powder
1 T. baking powder
¾ t. baking soda
¾ t. salt
¾ c. strong coffee-hot
¾ c. hot water
1 ½ c. buttermilk
¼ c. canola oil
4 eggs
1 t. vanilla

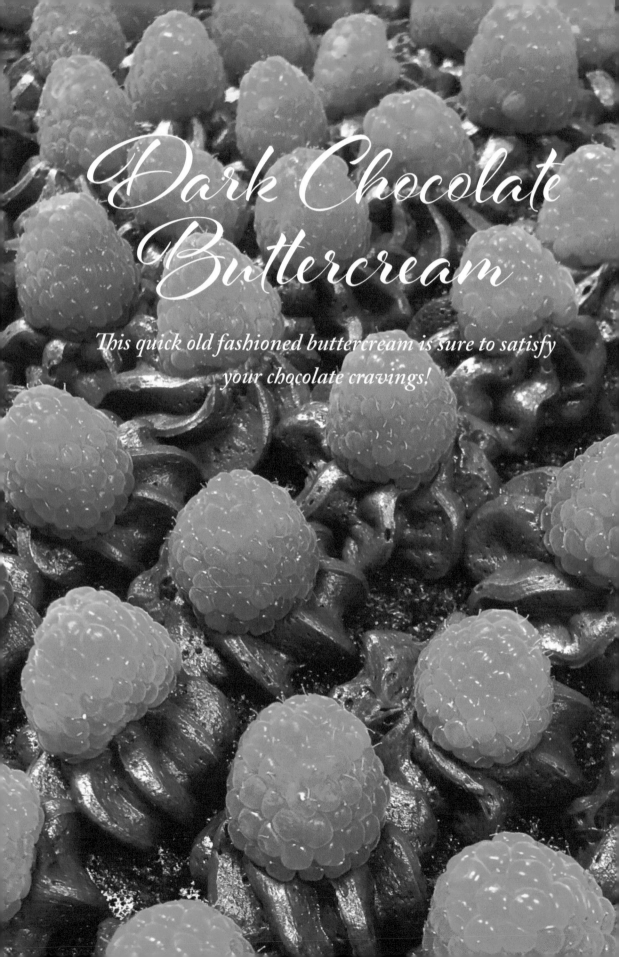

Dark Chocolate Buttercream

This quick old fashioned buttercream is sure to satisfy your chocolate cravings!

Method:

In kitchen aid with paddle attachment on low speed or large mixing bowl with a wooden spoon, cream butter until smooth with powdered sugar and cocoa powder.

Slowly add half and half until frosting comes together in a ball and then turn up speed and beat icing until smooth and creamy, adding vanilla and more half and half if needed to reach desired consistency.

Buttercream should be soft enough to spread on cake but not runny so it is better to add the liquid slowly rather than all at once.

Frosts a triple layer 9 inch cake.

Dark Chocolate Buttercream

Ingredients:

**1½ pounds sifted powdered sugar
¾ c. dark cocoa powder
6 ounces unsalted butter-
  softened
½ c. half and half
1 t. vanilla extract**

Pipe Buttercream on to Dark Chocolate Cake and top with fresh raspberries for a spectacular dessert!

I intend that my last work shall be a cookbook composed of memories and desires.

– Author: Alexandre Dumas

Tender Butter Cake

*I use this recipe for my Old Fashioned Coconut Cake
and it is always a crowd pleaser!*

Method:

Line 3-9" cake pans with parchment paper and spray lightly with Pam.

Sift together dry ingredients and set aside.

In mixing bowl with electric beaters or kitchen aid with paddle attachment cream together butter and sugar with vanilla until light and fluffy.

Slowly add egg yolks and beat well. Scrape down sides and bottom of bowl with rubber spatula, do this after every addition!

Now, add half the dry ingredients and mix on low until incorporated then add all the yoghurt, mix and scrape down sides before adding the remaining dry ingredients.

Mix on low until incorporated then increase speed to medium high and beat 2-3 minutes. In a separate bowl whip egg whites until stiff peaks form.

Fold a third of the beaten egg whites into the batter with a rubber spatula then add remaining whites, folding until incorporated and no streaks of whites remain. This requires a light hand, fold whites into batter gently, trying to keep as much air into batter as possible.

Divide into the three pans and bake 25-30 minutes or until lightly golden brown and toothpick comes out clean when inserted in middle of cake.

Cool completely before removing from pans and frost with creamy vanilla buttercream.

Old Fashioned Coconut Cake

Finish cake with angel flake coconut pressed into sides and top for the best Easter cake ever!

Tender Butter Cake

Pre-heat oven to 350°

Ingredients:

**8 ounces unsalted butter - softened
3 c. sugar
6 eggs separated
8 ounces plain yoghurt
2 c. cake flour
1 c. all purpose flour
1/2 t. baking soda
1/2 t. salt
1 t. vanilla extract**

Zoey's Cream Puffs

Method:

Line a baking sheet pan with parchment paper and set aside.

Place milk, butter and salt in medium saucepan over medium-high heat. Bring to a scald, stirring occasionally until butter is melted and to prevent burning. Add flour all at once and stir vigorously with a wooden spoon over heat until mixture balls together and is smooth, about one minute or so. Remove from heat and transfer dough to kitchen aid with paddle attachment or mixing bowl with electric beaters. While still hot start mixing dough on medium speed adding eggs one at a time until incorporated. Continue beating, increasing speed to high until mixture is smooth and glossy. Spoon batter into pastry bag and pipe half dollar sized mounds onto parchment lined pan, allowing space between puffs to expand. Lightly smooth tops with your finger if there are any uneven peaks from piping bag. Bake for 15 minutes on 400 degrees then turn pan around in oven and reduce heat to 325 degrees for another 15 minutes. They should puff up and be golden brown on the outside and light and airy on the inside. This recipe yields about 18 puffs.

To finish:

Make ganache by bringing 1/2 c. heavy cream to a boil in small saucepan, remove from heat and whisk in 1 c. dark chocolate chips until smooth, set aside.

Whip 12 ounces heavy cream with 6-8 Tablespoons powdered sugar and 1/2 t. vanilla. Slice top off cream puffs with a serrated knife and pipe cream generously into bottom half. Dip tops into dark chocolate ganache and place on top of filled cream puff. Enjoy!

Zoey's Cream Puffs

Pre-heat oven to 400°

**First, make the puffs.
This dough is called Paté
Choux and is the base
for eclairs also.
Special equipment:
pastry bag**

Paté Choux ingredients:
1 c. milk
4 ounces unsalted butter
½ t. salt
1 c. flour
4 eggs

Filling and Topping;
16 ounces heavy cream
**6-8 Tablespoons
powdered sugar**
½ t. vanilla
1 c. dark chocolate chips
1 t. vanilla extract

Vegan Chocolate Cake with Dark Chocolate Glaze

Method:

Sift dry ingredients together and place in mixing bowl with electric beaters or Kitchen Aid with paddle attachment.

On low speed slowly add the hot coffee, soy milk and canola oil, scraping down sides of bowl making sure all dry ingredients have been absorbed by the liquid.

Add the vanilla and vinegar, increase speed to medium high and beat 2-3 minutes.

Pour batter into greased and parchment paper lined pan and bake 35-40 minutes or until top lightly springs back when touched and cake starts to pull slightly away from sides of pan.

Cool before removing in pan or you can leave it in the pan to glaze, either way is fine. Top with glaze when cool and let set at least 30 minutes before serving.

To Make glaze:

Place sugar and cocoa in mixing bowl and whisk to combine. Add corn syrup, vanilla and hot water, whisking vigorously. Add water slowly until a spreadable consistency is reached. Pour over cake and spread to sides with an offset spatula.

Note: This recipe has been adapted from Madhuram's vegan chocolate cake recipe.

This vegan chocolate cake keeps moist for days.

Vegan Chocolate Cake with Dark Chocolate Glaze

Pre-heat oven to 350°

9 inch square pan

Ingredients:
1 ½c. all purpose flour
1 c. sugar
½ t. salt
1 t. baking soda
1/3 c. cocoa powder
2 t. vanilla
⅓ c. canola oil
¼ c. hot coffee
¾ c. soy milk
1 T. apple cider or white vinegar

Dark Chocolate glaze Ingredients:

1 c. powdered sugar-sifted
¼ c. dark cocoa powder-sifted
2 T. light corn syrup
½ t. vanilla
Hot water, about ⅛ to ¼ c.

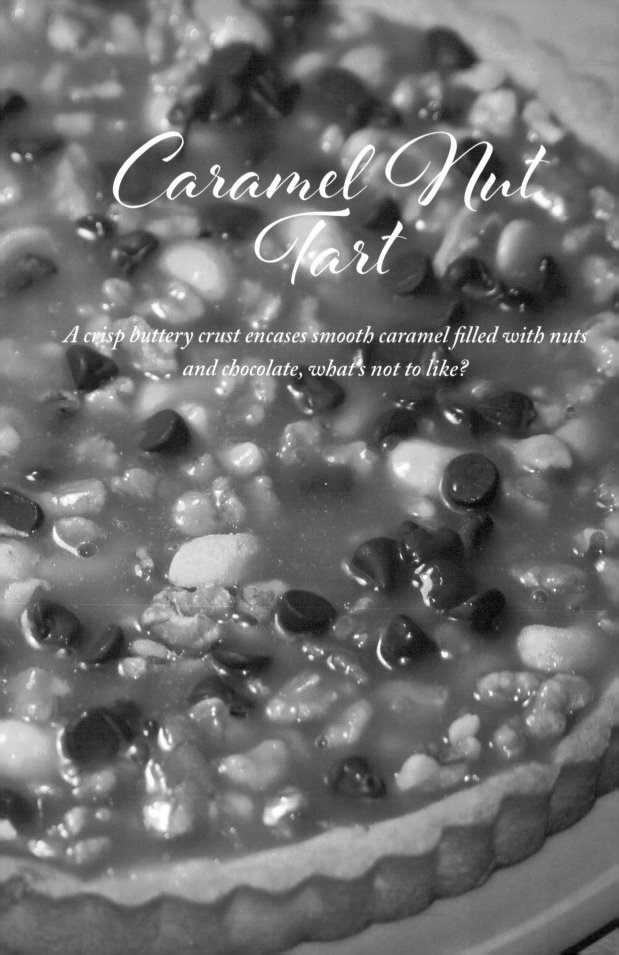

Caramel Nut Tart

A crisp buttery crust encases smooth caramel filled with nuts and chocolate, what's not to like?

Method:

Cream together butter and powdered sugar until smooth, add egg and mix well. Stir in flour and salt just until dough is mixed through and smooth. Divide into two rounds, flatten into discs and wrap in plastic. Refrigerate at least one hour before rolling out dough. This recipe makes 2 large tart shells so you can freeze one for later use. On a lightly floured board, roll out dough to fit a 9 inch tart shell. Lightly spray tart shell with Pam before placing dough into it, pressing dough into sides and bottom of pan before trimming off any excess over top. Chill in freezer for 10 minutes before baking at 350 degrees for 15-20 minutes or until lightly golden brown around top and edges. When cool, fill with nuts and chocholate and set aside.

To make carmel:

In a medium sized saucepan over high heat melt corn syrup with sugar, stirring until dissolved. When sugar reaches a golden brown color turn off heat and slowly pour in cream while stirring caramel with a large wooden spoon. Be careful, caramel will bubble up and create steam so it's wise to wear an oven mitt when doing this. Stir in butter and vanilla returning to heat for one minute and stirring until smooth. Transfer caramel to a heat proof Pyrex or metal measuring cup and pour slowly over nut and chocolate mixture. Cool completely before cutting. Serves 8.

Caramel Nut Tart

Pre-heat oven to 350°

For the crust:
8 ounces unsalted butter
1½ c. powdered sugar
1 egg
3 c.+2 T. flour
½ t. salt

For filling:
2 c. Pecan or walnut pieces
½ c. Dark chocolate chunks
Place nuts and chocolate in pre-baked tart shell, set aside

Caramel Ingredients:
4 T. corn syrup
1 ¼ c. sugar
¾ c. heavy cream
2 T. unsalted butter
1 t. vanilla
Pinch of salt

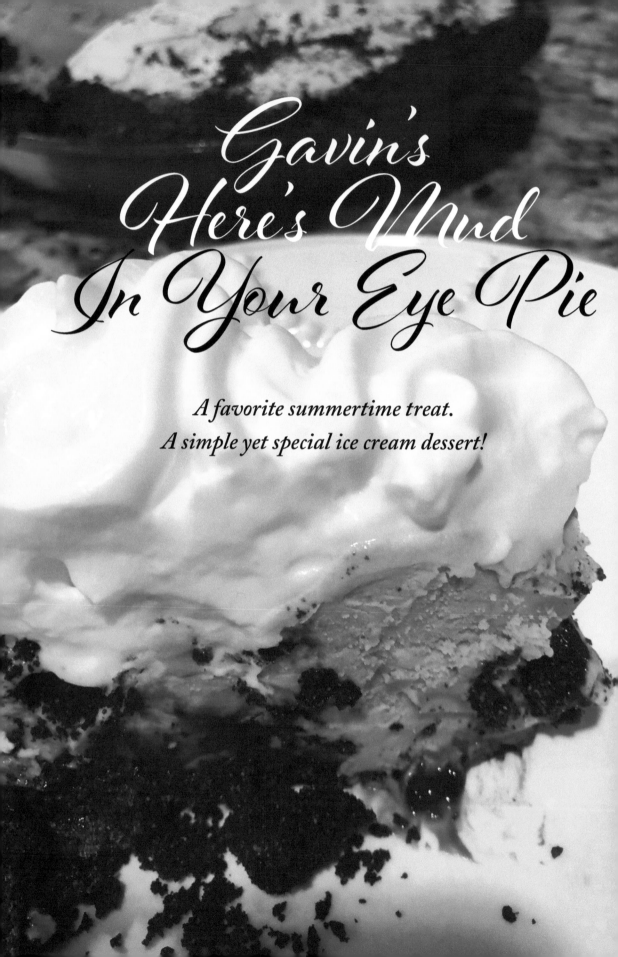

Gavin's
Here's Mud
In Your Eye Pie

A favorite summertime treat.
A simple yet special ice cream dessert!

Method:

Spoon hot fudge sauce (NOT HEATED) into the bottom of the Oreo cookie pie crust. Scoop ice cream on top of the fudge sauce, this works better if slightly softened. Press down ice cream evenly with back of spoon. Place in freezer for at least one hour before topping with sweetened whipped cream. Top with sprinkles or chocolate shavings if desired.

Serves 8.

Here's Mud In Your Eye Pie

Ingredients:

Oreo cookie crumb pie shell - available in the baking aisle of your supermarket
1 jar of hot fudge sauce
1½ quarts coffee or vanilla ice cream
1 c. heavy whipping cream
4 T. powdered sugar

Method:

Sift together all the dry ingredients and set aside.

In a kitchen aid mixer with paddle attachment on medium speed, cream together the 8 ounces butter and brown sugar until light, add eggs one at a time and cream until light and fluffy, making sure to scrape down sides of bowl and bottom to ensure even mixing. Reduce speed to low and add half of the dry ingredients, mixing just until incorporated. Add milk and vanilla slowly to batter, scrape down sides and mix until batter is smooth. Add remaining flour and mix just until incorporated. Stop and scrape down sides and bottom of bowl then return to medium speed, mixing for one minute.

To bake:

Scoop batter out with one ounce ice cream scoop onto parchment lined baking sheets, this will make 48 cookies, you'll need 2 cookies to make one pie, which will give you 2 dozen pies. Space 12 balls evenly on sheet tray and with moistened finger tips press down lightly on each one, this helps them stay in place and spread out evenly, do this lightly, no need to flatten them out! Bake each tray 8-10 minutes at 350 degrees, rotating tray halfway through baking to ensure an even bake. Remove from oven and let cool. Peel off cookies from parchment paper and generously spread filling on the bottom of one cookie, sandwich together with bottom of another cookie and let sit on flat surface to set. They keep well in a Tupperware container for 3-4 days.

Whoopie Pies

This recipe yields 2 dozen "pies"

Pre-heat oven to 350°
Special tools- 1 ounce ice cream scoop, piping bag for filling (optional);

Ingredients for cookie-pies:
8 ounces unsalted butter
2 c. dark brown sugar
4 eggs
3 c. flour
1 t. salt
2 t. baking soda
1 c. cocoa powder
1 c. milk
1 t. vanilla

For filling:
8 ounces unsalted butter
2 c. powdered sugar- sift after measuring
2 c. marshmallow fluff

To make filling:

Cream the butter until light and then add the sifted powdered sugar, mixing just until incorporated. Add marshmallow fluff and beat until smooth and creamy. You can spread this filling onto cookie-pies with a spatula or use a piping bag (I recommend this method, less messy and easier to control) to fill cookie-pies. Enjoy!

Almond Raspberry Tart

Method:

To make crust:

Cream together butter and powdered sugar until smooth, add egg and mix well. Stir in flour and salt just until dough is mixed through and smooth. Divide into two rounds, flatten into discs and wrap in plastic. Refrigerate at least one hour before rolling out dough. This recipe makes 2 large tart shells so you can freeze one for later use. On a lightly floured board, roll out dough to fit a 9 inch tart shell. Lightly spray tart shell with Pam before placing dough into it, pressing dough into sides and bottom of pan before trimming off any excess over top. Chill in freezer for 10 minutes before baking at 350 degrees for 15-20 minutes or until lightly golden brown around top and edges.

To make filling:

In kitchen aid with paddle attachment or by hand in mixing bowl cream together the almond paste and sugar until crumbly. Add butter and mix until smooth. Beat in eggs, vanilla and salt until mixture is light and creamy, add flour and beat one minute until incorporated.

To assemble tart:

Place a spoonful of raspberry jam on bottom of partially cooked tart shell. Fill a piping bag with the almond filling and pipe into shell using a circular motion starting from outer edges in, covering jam completely. Dot top of filling with raspberries and sprinkle with almonds. Bake at 350 for about 30-40 minutes for small tarts and 60 minutes for larger size, top will be golden brown. Remove from oven and cool, dust with powdered sugar and enjoy!

Almond Raspberry Tart

One 9 in. tart or 6 individual tarts

Pre-heat oven to 350°

For the crust:
8 ounces unsalted butter
1 ½ c. powdered sugar
1 egg
3 c.+2 T. flour
½ t. salt

Filling:
6 ounces almond paste
6 ounces organic cane sugar
6 ounces unsalted butter
1 t. vanilla
¼ t. salt
3 eggs
½ c. unbleached organic flour

Additional ingredients:
Raspberry jam
Fresh raspberries
Sliced almonds
Powdered sugar

Most of us have fond memories of food from our childhood. Whether it was our mom's homemade lasagna or a memorable chocolate birthday cake, food has a way of transporting us back to the past.
– Author: Homaro Cantu

Photographer Richard Lancaster perusing the selections at Bart's Books.

Ojai was used as the setting for the mystical "Shangri La" in the 1937 film Lost Horizon. Over the years its beauty and special atmosphere has been a draw for artists, musicians and spiritual seekers from all over the world.

CPSIA information can be obtained
at www.ICGtesting.com
Printed in the USA
BVHW021942050722
641272BV00002B/23